# ESSEX
## Wit & Humour

CAMILLA ZAJAC

BRADWELL
BOOKS

Published by Bradwell Books
9 Orgreave Close Sheffield S13 9NP
Email: books@bradwellbooks.co.uk
Complied by Camilla Zajac

British Library Cataloguing in Publication Data: a catalogue record for
this book is available
from the British Library.

1st Edition

ISBN: 9781902674681

Print: Gomer Press, Llandysul, Ceredigion SA44 4JL
Design by: jenksdesign@yahoo.co.uk
Illustrations: ©Tim O'Brien 2013

**A farmer from** Epping was ploughing his field, looked around and saw a visiting parson at the gate.

So on next his circuit he stopped to pay his respects.

'My, but you and God have built a beautiful place together' said the parson.

'You're right, Parson. replied the Farmer, "But between you and me, you should have see it when he had it all to himself'.

**A cocky young** man working on a building site in Braintree was bragging that he could outdo anyone in a feat of strength. He made a special case of making fun of Morris, one of the older workmen. After several minutes, Morris had had enough.

'Why don't you put your money where your mouth is?' he said. 'I will bet a week's wages that I can haul something in a wheelbarrow over to that outbuilding that you won't be able to wheel back.'

'You're on, old man,' the boaster replied. 'It's a bet! Let's see what you got.'

Morris reached out and grabbed the wheelbarrow by the handles. Then, nodding to the young man, he said, 'All right. Get in.'

**Harry proudly drove** his new convertible into town and parked it on the main street, he was on his way to the Charity Shop to get rid of an unwanted gift, a foot spa, which he left on the back seat.

He had walked half way down the street when he realised that he had left the top down... with the foot spa in the back.

He ran all the way back to his car, but it was too late...

Another five foot spas had been dumped in the car.


**Did you hear** about the two men from the monastery who opened up a seafood restaurant? One was the fish friar, and the other was the chip monk.

**There was a** competition to cross the English Channel doing the breast-stroke and the three women who entered the race were named Emily, Maggie and Rose, all from Essex.

After approximately 14 hours, Emily staggered up on the shore and was declared the fastest. About 40 minutes later, Maggie crawled up on the shore and was declared the second place finisher.

Nearly 4 hours after that, Rose finally came ashore and promptly collapsed in front of the worried onlookers.

When the reporters asked why it took her so long to complete the race, she replied, 'I don't want to sound like I'm a poor loser, but I think those two other girls were using their arms.'

**A couple from** Manningtree had been courting for nearly twenty years and one day as they sat on a seat in the park, the woman plucked up courage and asked,
'Don't you think it's time we wed?'
He answered,
'Yes, but who'd have us?'

**Did you hear** about the man who was convicted of stealing luggage from Stanstead airport?

He asked for twenty other cases to be taken into account.

## Unusual Essex place names

- Bachelors Bump
- Pork Lane
- Turkey Cock Lane
- Ugley
- Chignall Smealy
- Fingringhoe
- Good Easter
- Layer-de-la-Haye
- Messing.

**A man walks** into a bookshop and says 'I hope you don't have a book on reverse psychology.'

**Did you hear** that they've crossed a Newfoundland and a Basset Hound? The new breed is a Newfound Asset Hound, a dog for financial advisors.

**How many surrealists** does it take to screw in a lightbulb? Banana.

**How do you** make an Essex omelette?
First nick three eggs...


**Two old ladies** in Boxted were having a chat. One says to the other, 'You can tell winter's on its way because the butter's 'ard '.

**An Englishman, Irishman** and a Scotsman walk into a bar.
The Barman says 'Is this a joke?'

You can have me but cannot hold me:
Gain me and quickly lose me.
If treated with care I can be great.
And if betrayed I will break.
What am I?

Trust.

Six dozen dozen is greater than half a dozen dozen — yes or no?

No, both are equal.

**A scruffy looking** man went into a jewellers shop in Clacton. The first thing the sales girl noticed was his exaggerated chewing.

'Can I help you, Sir?'

'Yes' he said, chopping away. 'I'd like one of them there rings'.

'Yes Sir, wedding or engagement?'

'Wedding', he said, gurning away.

'Gold or Silver?' asked the salesgirl, watching him with increasing disgust.

'Gold', he replied.

'Eighteen carats?' said the girl.

'No, luv. I've toffee stuck in me teeth'.

**A life-long** city man, tired of the rat race in his home town of Basildon, decided he was going to give up the city life, move to the country, and become a chicken farmer. He bought an organic chicken farm in a rural part of Essex and moved in. It turned out that his next door neighbour was also a chicken farmer. The neighbour came for a visit one day and said, 'Chicken farming isn't easy. I know. To help you get started, I'll give you 100 chickens.'

The new chicken farmer was delighted. Two weeks later the neighbour dropped by to see how things were going. The new farmer said, 'Not too well mate. All 100 chickens died.' The neighbour said, 'Oh, I can't believe that. I've never had any trouble with my chickens. I'll give you 100 more.' Another two weeks went by and the neighbour dropped in again. The new farmer said, 'You're not going to believe this, but the second 100 chickens died too.' Astounded, the neighbour asked, 'What went wrong?' The new farmer said, 'Well, I'm not sure whether I'm planting them too deep or too close together.'

**At an antiques** auction in Brentwood, a wealthy American announced that he had lost his wallet containing £5,000, and would give a reward of £50 to the person who found it. From the back of the hall came a shout, 'I'll give £100!'

**Stan and Alf** worked in a sawmill in Epping Forest. Alf is very accident-prone. One day Alf slipped and his arm got caught and severed by the saw. Stan quickly puts the arm in a plastic bag and rushes it and Alf to the local hospital. Next day, Stan goes to the hospital and asks about Alf. The nurse replies, 'Oh he's fine, we've reattached his arm'. The very next day he's back at work in the sawmill.

Within a couple of days Alf has another accident and severs his head. Stan puts the head in a plastic bag and transports it and Alf to the hospital. Next day he went in and asks the nurse how Alf is. The nurse breaks down and cries and says, 'He's dead'. Stan is shocked, but not surprised, and says to the nurse: 'I suppose the saw finally did him in'.

'No', says the nurse, 'Some idiot put his head in a plastic bag and he suffocated'.

**At a pub** in Colchester, a newcomer asks a local ....
'Have you lived here all your life?'

After a long pause the man replies 'Don't know yet!'

**A tourist in** a shop in Canvey Island, 'Have you got anything in the shape of motor car tyres?' Shopkeeper: 'Oh, yes. We've got lifebuoys, invalid cushions, funeral wreaths and doughnuts.'

**What do you** do if you are driving your car in central London and you see a space man?

Park in it, of course.

**A group of** chess enthusiasts checked into a hotel and were standing in the lobby discussing their recent tournament victories. After about an hour, the manager came out of the office and asked them to move. 'But why?' they asked, as they walked off. 'Because,' he said 'I can't stand chess nuts boasting in an open foyer.'

What walks all day on its head?

A nail in a horse shoe.

**Have you heard** about the latest machine on the pier at Clacton on Sea?

You put ten pence in and ask it any question and it gives you a true answer.
One holiday maker from Colchester tried it last week.

He asked the machine 'Where is my father?' The machine replied:
'Your father is fishing in Lowestoft.'

Well, he thought, that's daft for a start because my father is dead.
'Where is my mother's husband?'

Back came the reply, 'Your mother's husband is buried in Chelmsford, but your father is still fishing in Lowestoft.'

**After a night** out on the town in Basildon, Bill was struggling to get home one night, after having had a few drinks when he saw a man from the water board with a big 'T' handle, in the middle of the road opening a valve at the bottom of a manhole.

He walked up behind him and gave him a big shove.

'What's that for?' said the waterman...

'That's for turning all the streets round when I'm trying to find my way home!'

**A father and** his son, Bobby, arrive at the local football match in Colchester and Dad can't find the tickets. Dad: 'Nip home and see if I left the tickets there.' Bobby: 'No probs, Dad.' Half an hour later Bobby returns to his dad who is patiently waiting outside the football pitch. Bobby: 'Yep, they're on the kitchen table where you left them.'

My life can be measured in hours:
I serve by being devoured.
Thin. I am quick; fat. I am slow.
Wind is my foe.
What am I?

A candle.

**They say an** Englishman laughs three times at a joke. The first time when everybody gets it, the second a week later when he thinks he gets it, the third time a month later when somebody explains it to him.

**Two aerials meet** on a roof - fall in love - get married. The ceremony was rubbish - but the reception was brilliant.

**A man went** into a hardware store and asked to buy a sink.
'Would you like one with a plug?' asked the assistant.
'Don't tell me they've gone electric,' said the man.

I give you a group of three. One is sitting down and will never get up. The second eats as much as is given to him, yet is always hungry. The third goes away and never returns. What are they?

A stove, fire and smoke.

A man enters a dark cabin. He has just one match with him. There is an oil lamp, a wood stove, and a fireplace in the cabin. What would he light first?

The match.

**A boy from** Dagenham started school and his dad gave him two pounds for the bus home. Instead of getting on the bus the boy decides to run behind it all the way home. Dad comes home from the pub and the boy says, 'Dad I saved you two quid today because I ran behind the bus instead of getting on'.

The dad sends him to bed without supper saying, 'You should have run behind a taxi and saved me 40 quid you little...'

**Why couldn't Cinderella** be a good soccer player?
She lost her shoe, she ran away from the ball, and her coach was a pumpkin.

**What do you** call a boomerang that won't come back?
A stick.

**What is the longest** word in the English language?
Smiles. Because there is a mile between its first and last letters.

What is it that never asks you any questions and yet you answer?

Your phone.

Your mother's brother's only brother-in-law is your Stepfather,
Grandfather, Uncle or Father?

Your Father.

**A London lawyer** and a man from Colchester were sitting next to each other on a long flight to Stansted. The lawyer is mistakenly thinking that Essex men are easily fooled

So the lawyer asks if the man would like to play a fun game.
The man is tired and just wants to take a nap. He politely declines and tries to catch a few winks. The lawyer persists and says that the game is a lot of fun.

'I ask you a question, and if you don't know the answer, you pay me only £5; you ask me one, and if I don't know the answer, I will pay you £500.'
This catches the man's attention and he agrees to play the game.
The lawyer asks the first question. 'What's the distance from the Earth to the moon?'

The man doesn't say a word, reaches in his pocket, pulls out a five-pound note, and hands it to the lawyer.

Now, it's the Essex man's turn. He asks the lawyer, 'What goes up a hill with three legs, and comes down with four?'

The lawyer uses his laptop, searches all the references he knows. He uses the air-phone; he searches the web and even the British Library. He sends emails to all the clever friends he knows, all to no avail. After over an hour of searching, he finally gives up.

He wakes up the man and hands him £500 which he pockets and goes straight back to sleep.

The lawyer is going crazy not knowing the answer. He woke his fellow passenger up again and asks, 'Well! What goes up a hill with three legs and comes down with four?'

He reaches in his pocket, hands the lawyer £5 and goes back to sleep.

**What do you** call an '80s synth pop band crossed with a scoop of ice cream?

Depeche a la Mode.

(The band Depeche Mode was formed in Basildon, Essex!)

**Who gives crocodiles** presents on Christmas?
Santa Jaws!

(The first crocodile to be brought to the UK arrived in 1701, transported by Richard Bradley who kept it in the lake at his home in Braintree, Essex!)

**A passenger in** a taxi tapped the driver on the shoulder to ask him something.

The driver screamed, lost control of the cab, nearly hit a bus, drove up over the curb and stopped just inches from a large plate glass window. For a few moments everything was silent in the cab, then the driver said, 'Please, don't ever do that again. You scared the daylights out of me.'

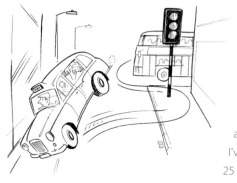

The passenger, who was also frightened, apologised and said he didn't realize that a tap on the shoulder could frighten him so much, to which the driver replied, 'I'm sorry, it's really not your fault at all. Today is my first day driving a cab. I've been driving a hearse for the last 25 years.'

A girl who was just learning to drive went down a one-way street in the wrong direction, but didn't break the law. How come?

She was walking.

A man builds a house rectangular in shape. All the sides have southern exposure. A big bear walks by. What colour is the bear? Why?

The bear is white because the house is built on the North Pole.

**Last night the** wife and I walked past a swanky new restaurant in Braintree ...

... 'Did you smell that food?"'she asked... 'Wonderful!'

Being the kind hearted, generous man that I am, I thought,

'What the hell, I'll treat her!

So we walked past it a second time.

What comes once in a minute, twice in a moment, but never in a thousand years?

The letter M.

**A new client** had just come in to see a famous lawyer.

'Can you tell me how much you charge?', said the client.

'Of course', the lawyer replied, 'I charge £200 to answer three questions!'

'Well that's a bit steep, isn't it?'

'Yes it is,' said the lawyer, 'And what's your third question?'

**What kind of** ears does an engine have?

Engineers

I am so small, and sometimes I'm missed.
I get misplaced, misused, and help you when you list.
People usually pause when they see me.
So can you tell me what I could be?

A comma.

When one does not know what it is, then it is something; but when one knows what it is, then it is nothing?

A riddle.

**A man walks** into a bank in Harwich and asks for a loan.

He tells the bank manager he is going to Australia on business for two weeks and needs to borrow £5,000.

The bank manager tells the customer that the bank will need some form of security for the loan, so the man hands over the keys and documents of new Ferrari parked on the street in front of the bank. He produces the log book and everything checks out.

The bank manager agrees to accept the car as collateral for the loan.

The bank manager and his staff are bemused by the casually dressed man using a £120,000 Ferrari as collateral against a £5000 loan.

The bank manager then instructs an employee of the bank to park the Ferrari in the bank's underground garage.

Two weeks later, the man returns, repays the £5,000 and the interest of £15.41.

The manager says to the customer, 'Sir, we are very happy to have had your business and this transaction has worked out very nicely, but we are a little puzzled.

While you were away, we checked you out further and found that you are a multi-millionaire.

What puzzles us is, why would you bother to borrow £5,000?'

The customer replies: 'Where else in Colchester can I park my car for two weeks for only £15.41 and expect it to be there when I return?'

**Many years ago** there was a dispute between two villages' one in Essex and the other in Suffolk; one day the villagers hear the cry "One Essex man is stronger than one hundred Suffolk men."

The villagers in Suffolk are incensed and immediately send their 100 strongest men to engage with the enemy; they are horrified by the screams and shouts. After hours of fighting all is quiet and non return. Later the same voice shouts out, "Is that the best you can do?"

This fires up the people from Suffolk and they rally round and get 1000 men to do battle; after days of the most frightful blood curling sounds one man emerged from the battlefield, barely able to speak but with his last breath manages to murmur "It's a trap, there's two of them!"

**A man wanted** to become a monk so he went to the monastery and talked to the head monk.

The head monk said, 'You must take a vow of silence and can only say two words every three years.'

The man agreed and after the first three years, the head monk came to him and said, 'What are your two words?'

'Food cold!' the man replied.

Three more years went by and the head monk came to him and said 'What are your two words?'

'Robe dirty!' the man exclaimed.

Three more years went by and the head monk came to him and said, 'What are your two words?'

'I quit!' said the man.

'Well', the head monk replied, 'I'm not surprised. You've done nothing but complain ever since you got here!'

What has five eyes, but cannot see?

The Mississippi River.

What was given to you, belongs to you exclusively and yet is used more by your friends than by yourself?

Your name.

"Brothers and sisters have I none, yet that man's father is my father's son" who is "that man"?

That man is your son.

**Albert a farmer** from Coggeshall is visited by Ken a farmer from Framlingham.

Ken. 'How big is your farm?'

Albert. 'See those trees over there? That's the boundary of my farmland.'

Ken. 'Hell, it takes me three days to drive to the boundary of my farm.'

Albert. 'I had a car like that once.'

**A duck walks** into a pub and goes up to the barman.

The barman says 'What can I get you?'

Duck: 'Umm. Do you have any grapes?'

Barman (Looking surprised):
'No, I'm afraid we don't.'

The duck waddles slowly out of the pub.

The next day at the same time, the duck waddles into the pub, hops up on a bar stool.

Barman: 'Hi. What can I get for you?'

Duck: 'Um. Do you have any grapes?'

Barman (a little annoyed): 'Hey! Weren't you in here yesterday. Look mate, we don't have any grapes. OK?'

The duck hops off the stool and waddles out of the door.

The next day, at the same time, the barman is cleaning some glasses when he hears a familiar voice

Duck: 'Umm.. Do you have any grapes?'

The barman is really annoyed

Barman: 'Look. What's your problem? You came in here yesterday asking for grapes, I told you, we don't have any grapes! Next time I see your little ducktail waddle in here I'm going to nail those little webbed feet of yours to the floor. GOT me pal?'

So the duck hops off the bar stool and waddles out.
The next day at the same time, the duck waddles into the pub, walks up to the barman and the barman says,

'What on earth do YOU want?'

'Errrr. do you have any nails?'

'What!? Of course not.'

'Oh. Well, do you have any grapes?'

**Did you hear** about the truck driver from Witham who was seen desperately chiselling away at the brickwork after his lorry got stuck while passing through a tunnel?

'Why don't you let some air out of your tyres?' asked a friendly passer-by.

'No, mate,' replied the driver 'it's the roof that won't go under, not the wheels'.

What gets wetter and wetter the more it dries?

A towel.

What goes around the world but stays in a corner?

A stamp.

What has a head like a cat, feet like a cat, a tail like a cat, but isn't a cat?

A kitten.

**A man from** Clacton phoned his son in Carlisle three days before Christmas and says, 'I hate to ruin your day but I have to tell you that your mother and I are divorcing; forty-five years of misery is enough.'

'Dad, what are you talking about?' the son screams.

'We can't stand the sight of each other any longer' the father says. 'We're sick of each other and I'm sick of talking about this, so you call your sister in Bristol and tell her.'

Frantic, the son calls his sister, who explodes on the phone. 'Like hell they're getting divorced!' she shouts, 'I'll take care of this!'

She calls her father immediately, and screams at him 'You are NOT getting divorced. Don't do a single thing until I get there. I'm calling my brother back, and we'll both be there tomorrow. Until then, don't do a thing, DO YOU HEAR ME?'' and hangs up.

The old man hangs up his phone and turns to his wife. 'Sorted! They're coming for Christmas - and they're paying their own way.'

**Two boys were** arguing when the teacher entered the room.

The teacher says, 'Why are you arguing?'

One boy answers, 'We found a ten pound note and decided to give it to whoever tells the biggest lie.

'You should be ashamed of yourselves,' said the teacher, 'When I was your age I didn't even know what a lie was.'

The boys gave the ten pound note to the teacher.

**If vegetarians eat** vegetables, what do humanitarians eat?

**Two young lads** from Essex and their mate from over the border in Suffolk were at the fair and about to go on the helter-skelter when an old crone stepped in front of them.

'This is a magic ride,' she said. 'You will land in whatever you shout out on the way down.'

'I'm game for this,' says the first guy and slides down the helter-skelter shouting "GOLD!" at the top of his voice. Sure enough, when he hit the bottom he found himself surrounded by thousands of pounds worth of gold coins.

The next guy goes and he shouts "SILVER!" at the top of his voice. At the bottom he lands in more silver coinage than he can carry.

The man from Suffolk goes last and, launching himself from the top of the slide shouts "WEEEEEEE!"

**A man from** Thaxted bought two horses but he couldn't tell them apart. So he asked the farmer who lives next door what he should do.

The farmer suggests measuring them.

The man comes back triumphantly and says: 'The white horse is two inches taller than the black horse!'

I never was, am always to be.
No one ever saw me, nor ever will.
And yet I am the confidence of all
To live and breathe on this terrestrial ball.
What am I?

Tomorrow.

Light as a feather.
Nothing in it.
Few can hold it.
For even a minute.

Your breath.

**The leader of** a vegetarian society just couldn't control himself any more. He just needed to try some pork, just to see what it tasted like.

So one summer day he told his members he was going away for a break.

He left town and headed to the nearest restaurant. After sitting down, he ordered a roasted pig, and impatiently waited for his delicacy. After just a few minutes, he heard someone call his name, and to his horror he saw one of his fellow members walking towards him. Just at that same moment, the waiter walked over, with a huge platter, holding a full roasted pig with an apple in its mouth. 'Isn't that something,' says the man after only a moment's pause, 'All I do is order an apple, and look what it comes with!'

**A few years** ago, a little boy from Ashingdon, a small village in Essex, calls down to his mum from upstairs 'Mum! Muuum!'

'What's up Johnny?'

'Our Billy's taking all the overcoat for himself!'

(The Vicar had come to tea, the mother is embarrassed, and tries to make the best of things. She doesn't want the Vicar knowing she can't afford decent bedding...)

'Silly lad! It's called an 'eiderdown', not an overcoat!'
(A few minutes later)

A shout comes from upstairs - 'Mum! Muuum!'

'What's up now, Johnny?'

'Our Billy's pulled the sleeve off our eiderdown!'

**A man was** letting his dog run on a beach on Canvey Island when it led him across to a man buried up to his head in the sand, frantically calling for help....

He ran up and asked the man what had happened...The man said that some yobs had buried him for fun and he was so scared the tide would come in and drown him.

'Don't worry', said the first man, (as his dog licked the man's face) 'I'll run and get my shovel from the car and dig you out'.

'Is it a big one?' asked the buried man...

'Why do you ask?' said the dog owner...

'Well, you're going to need a big shovel.... I'm sitting on a donkey!'

**A man is** rushing to a hospital from a business trip because his wife has just gone into labour with twins, and there is a family tradition that the first family member to arrive gets to name the children. The man is afraid his wayward brother will show up first and give his kids horrible names.

When he finally arrives at the hospital in a cold sweat he sees his brother sitting in the waiting room, waving, with a silly grin on his face. He walks unhappily in to see his wife who is scowling and holding two little babies, a boy and a girl. Almost afraid to hear it, the man asks, 'What did he name the girl?' 'Denise' says the wife. 'Hey that's not too bad! What did he name the boy?' 'De-nephew.'

**A man from** Courtsend fell out with his in-laws and banned them from entering the house while he was in it. The wife faithfully carried out his wishes until she was on her death bed and then asked sadly, 'I've always been a good wife to you, haven't I, Jack?' 'Yes, my dear. None better,' he replied. 'Then I hope that you will grant my last request and let our Mary Alice ride in the first car with you at my funeral?' 'Alright my dear,' he agreed heavily, 'But I'm warning you, it'll spoil all my fun!'

**What lies at** the bottom of the ocean and twitches?

A nervous wreck.

**What's the difference** between roast beef and pea soup?

Anyone can roast beef.

What kind of coat can only be put on when wet?

A coat of paint.

What jumps when it walks and sits when it stands?

A kangaroo.

**There are many** good things to come out of Suffolk
- most of them roads into Essex.

**A man from** Dedham is walking along through the desert when he stumbles across an old lamp. He picks it up and rubs it and a genie appears before his eyes.

'You have two wishes,' the genie says 'Use them wisely.'

So the man says 'I want an everlasting Colchester Pudding!'

So the genie gives him the pudding.

The Essex man eats a bit of it then says 'Mmm that's good.

The genie asks 'What is your second wish?' without hesitation the man from Dedham replies – 'I'll have another one of these'.

**A man walks** into a doctor's office with two onions under his arms, a potato in his ear and a carrot up his nose. He asks the doctor: 'What's wrong with me?'

The doctor replies: 'You're not eating properly.'

**What time does** Sean Connery arrive at Wimbledon?
Tennish.

**Two blokes from** Billericay go into a pub.

Pint o'bitter, and a half o'shandy for my mate 'Donkey', please!

'Ere - what's with him calling you 'Donkey'?

Oh, 'e aw, 'e aw, 'e always calls me that!

**Local Police hunting** the 'Knitting Needle Nutter' who has stabbed six people in Essex in the last 48 hours, believe the attacker could be following some kind of pattern.

**A man ran** into a Colchester pub, bleeding heavily:

'Whose is that black Jaguar on the car park?'

**Did you hear** about the last wish of the henpecked husband of a house-proud Essex wife?

He asked to have his ashes scattered on the carpet.

What, when you need it you throw it away, but when you don't need it you take it back?

An anchor.

**Language student to** teacher, 'Are 'trousers' singular or plural?'
Teacher, 'They're singular on top and plural on the bottom.'

**Why was the** computer so tired when it got home?
Because it had a hard drive!

**What do you** get when you cross a dog with a telephone?
A Golden Receiver!

**What do cats** like to eat for breakfast?
Mice Krispies

**It's a quiet** night in Hatfield Heath a man and his wife are fast asleep when there is an unexpected knock on the door. He looks at his clock, its half past three in the morning. 'I'm not getting out of bed at this time,' he thinks, and rolls over.

A louder knock follows. 'Aren't you going to answer that?' says his wife. So the man dragged himself out of bed and went downstairs. He opened the door and there is strange man standing at the door. It didn't take the homeowner long to realise the man was drunk.

'Hi there,' slurs the stranger. 'Can you give me a push?'

"No, I'm sorry It's half past three. I was in bed,' said the man and slammed the door. He went back up to bed and told his wife what happened.

'That wasn't very nice of you,' she says.

'Remember that night we broke down in the pouring rain on the way to pick the kids up from the babysitter, and you had to knock on that man's door to get us started again? What would have happened if he'd told us to get lost?'

'But the guy was drunk,' replied the husband.

'Well we can at least help move his car somewhere safe and sort him out a taxi,' said his wife. 'He needs our help.' So the husband gets out of bed again, gets dressed, and goes downstairs. He opened the door, but couldn't to see the stranger anywhere, he shouts, 'Hey, do you still want a push?' And he hears a voice cry out, 'Yes please!' So, still being unable to see the stranger, he shouts,

'Where are you?'

'I'm over here,' the stranger replies, 'on your swing.'

**What gear were** you in at the moment of the impact?
Gucci sweats and Reeboks.

**What's green and** runs around the garden?
A hedge.

**How do you** make a sausage roll?
Push it!

**Missus! Your dog's** spoilt!

How dare you, sir!

No, it's spoilt. I ran over it with my truck...

Light as a feather.
Nothing in it.
Few can hold it.
For even a minute.

Your breath.

**Two men in** a butcher's shop in Chelmsford one of them says
'I bet you £100 that you can't reach that piece of meat on the ceiling'

The other man says 'I'm not betting!'

The first man says 'Why not?'

The other man says `The steaks are too high!'

**A depressed looking** man is sitting in a cheap, greasy diner in a Maldon suburb. He picks up the menu and sees that it contains just three dishes: meatloaf, shepherd's pie and Essex Hotpot. The waitress comes over to take his order. 'I'll have the Essex Hotpot,' says the man glumly, 'And if you could throw in a few kind words that would be very welcome.' The waitress leaves and returns a few minutes later with a plate of hotpot. She bangs the plate on the table in front of the man and starts to walk off. 'Hey,' says the man. 'I got my dinner; how about those kind words?' The waitress turns, takes the cigarette out her mouth and says, 'Don't eat the hotpot.'

**A Dagenham man** says to his wife, 'Get your coat on luv, I'm off to the club'.

His wife says, 'That's nice. You haven't taken me out for years'.

He says, 'You're not coming with me, I'm turning the heating off when I go out'.

**Why was the** scarecrow promoted?
He was outstanding in his field!

**What is the** longest word in the English language?
Smiles. Because there is a mile between its first and last letters.

**Two snowmen are** standing in a field. One says to the other 'That's funny, I can really smell carrots.'

**A man from** Danbury shouts urgently into the phone, 'My wife is pregnant, and her contractions are only two minutes apart!'

'Is this her first child?' the Doctor queries.

'No you idiot!' the man shouts. 'This is her husband!'

**What do the** donkeys at Leigh on Sea beach get for lunch? Half an hour!

**What does one** star say to another star when they meet?
Glad to meteor!

**What do you** get if you cross a nun and a chicken?
A pecking order!

What can you catch but not throw?

A cold.

**A man drove** past a country pub on the outskirts of Chelmsford and decided to go back in for a swift half. As he approached the front door he sees four old men sitting on a bench. 'Afternoon lads' says the bloke. The old men just mumbled something under their breaths in reply, so he went into the bar and ordered a pint. '1p says the barman. '1p, how come it's so cheap?' asks the punter. 'It's the 100th anniversary of the pub today and I'm celebrating by selling beer at the price it would have been when it opened' replies the barman. 'Great, but if you don't mind me asking, What's wrong with those lot on the bench?' says the guy. "Take no notice mate, they're upset 'cos I'm not having a happy hour'.

When I am filled.
I can point the way:
When I am empty.
Nothing moves me.
I have two skins.
One without and one within.
What am I?

A glove.

**In Braintree, a** woman and her husband heard a man driving down the road shouting 'The world is ending!'.

The wife said, 'Don't worry. It's only Farmer Geddon!'

**Bloke runs into** a pub in Billericay:
'Anyone got a large black cat with a white collar?'
'No!'

'Darn! I've run over the Vicar...'

**A farmer was** driving along a country road near Kelvedon with a large load of fertiliser. A little boy, playing in front of his house, saw him and called, 'What do you have in your truck?'

'Fertiliser,' the farmer replied.

'What are you going to do with it?' asked the little boy.

'Put it on strawberries,' answered the farmer.

'You ought to live here,' the little boy advised him. 'We put sugar and cream on ours.'

**A farmer and** his pig were driving down the road in High Roding when a policeman pulled him over. The policeman asked the farmer, 'Didn't you know it's against the law to ride with a pig in the cab of your tractor?'

The farmer replied, 'No, I didn't know that.' The cop asked the farmer where he was going and he said, 'To Leaden Roding.

The cop said, 'I'll let you off the hook this time if you promise to take the pig to a farm when you get to Leaden Roding.' So the farmer promised he would.

Several days later the policeman spotted the farmer with the pig driving down the road and pulled him over again. He said 'I thought I told you to take this pig to a farm when you got to Leaden Roding.'

The farmer replied, 'I did and we had so much fun, I'm taking him to a fair next!'

**Pete and Larry** hadn't seen each other in many years. They were having a long chat, telling each other all about their lives. Finally Pete invited Larry to visit him in his new apartment in Basildon. 'I have a wife and three kids and I'd love to have you visit us.'

'Great. Where do you live?'

'Here's the address. There's plenty of parking behind the flat. Park and come around to the front door, kick it open with your foot, go to the elevator and press the button with your left elbow, then enter! When you reach the sixth floor, go down the hall until you see my name on the door. Then press the doorbell with your right elbow and I'll let you in.'
'Great. But tell me...what is all this business of kicking the front door open, then pressing elevator buttons with my right, then my left elbow?'

Pete answered, "Surely you're not coming empty-handed?".

**Sam works in** an office in Dagenham, one day he walks into his boss's office and says, 'I'll be honest with you, I know the economy isn't great, but I have over three companies after me, and I would like to respectfully ask for a pay rise.'

After a few minutes of haggling, his manager finally agrees to a 5% raise, and Sam happily gets up to leave.

'By the way', asks the boss as Sam is getting up, 'Which three companies are after you?'

'The electric company, the water company, and the phone company', Sam replies.